Also by Charlie

POETRY

Red Roads

Indistinguishable from the Darkness

FICTION

Canaan

Shine Hawk

The Lives of the Dead

Crystal River

The Palms

The Palms

P o e m s

Charlie Smith

W. W. Norton & Company

New York   London

Copyright © 1993 by Charlie Smith

The text of this book is composed in 10/14 Electra
with the display set in Walbaum
Composition by Maple-Vail Composition Services
Manufacturing by Courier Companies, Inc.
Book design by Margaret Wagner

Library of Congress Cataloging-in-Publication Data

Smith, Charlie, 1947–
The palms / Charlie Smith.
p.   cm.
I. Title.
PS3569.M5163P34   1993
811'.54—dc20   92-21807

ISBN 0-393-03452-6

W.W. Norton & Company, Inc., 500 Fifth Avenue, New York, N.Y. 10110
W.W. Norton & Company Ltd., 10 Coptic Street, London WC1A 1PU

1 2 3 4 5 6 7 8 9 0

Acknowledgments

American Poetry Review: "The Bad Daughter," "The Hour of Our Birth"

Antioch Review: "My Parents' Wedding"

Boulevard: "Revision"

Columbia Magazine: "Omnipotence"

Crazyhorse: "Character Part"

Georgia Review: "The Fiddler"

Kenyon Review: "The Dogwood Tree"

The Nation: "Winter Door," "The White City"

New American Writing: "The Woman as Figure," "Some Don't Go South"

The New Yorker: "White Shining Sea," "Still Winter (Spring)," "Ice," "Mother at Eighty"

The Paris Review: "This Holy Enterprise," "Lies to the Dying," "To Lautreamont," "Chinese New Year"

Pequod: "Figurative Marriage"

Poetry East: "Jackplay"

Pivot: "Carnivore," "The Rose"

Sonora Review: "The Exile's Daughter"

Southern Poetry Review: "The Viewing," "Amnesia"

Threepenny Review: "The Palms"

Virginia Quarterly Review: "The Shaved Dog," "The Day Race"

Willow Springs: "Redneck Riviera," "Off-Season Repairs," "Kiss of the Moon," "The Childrens' House"

"The Woman as Figure" was reprinted in *The Best American Poetry, 1991*

Special thanks to Mark Rudman and Lawrence Joseph, and to Yaddo.

To Jill Bialosky

Contents

One *1*

My Parents' Wedding   *3*

This Holy Enterprise   *4*

The Woman as Figure   *5*

The Fiddler   *6*

The Palms   *7*

Figurative Marriage   *8*

Omnipotence   *10*

The Exile's Daughter   *11*

Jackplay   *13*

Character Part   *15*

Revision   *17*

Carnivore   *18*

Onanism   *20*

The Missing Person   *21*

Redneck Riviera   *22*

Lies to the Dying   *23*

The Day Race   *25*

Amnesia   *28*

On Hearing That a Hurricane Has Veered
Toward the States   *30*

The Shaved Dog   *32*

The Dogwood Tree   *34*

The Hour of Our Birth   *36*

T w o   37

White Shining Sea   39

The Viewing   41

Still Winter (Spring)   42

The Bad Daughter   43

The Ecstasies   44

"Out of Bitterness Comes Praise"   45

Some Don't Go South   48

Ice   49

Off-season Repairs   50

The Vivisectionist   51

Winter Door   52

Country Weekends   54

The White City   56

To Lautreamont   57

Chinese New Year   59

Lower Fifth   61

The Children's House   62

Kiss of the Moon   64

Mother at Eighty   65

Adhesion   66

Singapore   67

The Rose   69

One

My Parents' Wedding

I cannot believe how beautiful they are,
these two, beaming, like two prisoners escaped,
like Adam and Eve sneaked back into the Garden
and no God, no burning sword barring the way,
no terrible accusations and thunder, no rejection.
It's Hawaii, the war has come, the bougainvillea
shines like bodies turned inside out, the Scheffleras
that her mother cultivated in the dank halls
of the house on Moraine Street are twenty feet high,
there are roses beside the road, walls of them,
like a collection of corsages, and they are in love,
in the middle of it, in the middle of the strongest
country on earth arming itself, piling guns
into ships and on planes and in warehouses.
The docks are like ready carnivals,
and everyone has come, it is like a gathering
for some new election of the world's rulers, some port
of debarkation to another planet everyone is happy
to leave for, and they are in the middle of it,
madly in earnest, wild for each other's bodies, packed
with energy like the bombs the Japanese planes
twirled through gaps in the windward mountains.
Her hair is long and black and ripples like a river
and he is dressed in a white uniform; she is stretching
her body up to take his lips with hers, and it is one week
before he will find her in bed with his best friend.

This Holy Enterprise

The troubled entrepreneurs of evening—
the palm readers, the Mexican bracelet salesmen,
the girl who dances on a sheet of tin—
call out to me, turning for one second
their voices into instruments of love and attention,
promising love and attention, the Grail
of whatever singular prize I have longed for
and now found. I honor them all,
as I honor the priests
and the women who scream at the rain,
as I honor the envelope of bills and silver change
the boss hands me on Saturdays
saying *This is my body.* I have come around
to a pure absolution, gained—like a handful of grain
from the lords—by obedience, so that if I lie
all day Sunday like an effigy of myself,
harmless on the bed,
listening to the rants and vows
rising from the street, it is not because
I consider myself grandee of a greater enterprise,
but a child who listens at the door of his parents' room,
spellbound by the explanations they offer each other
of why the world moves
like a brutish uncle, drunk, through the house.
It is a tone I listen for, an inflection,
the moment when the argument breaks down
because someone can't take it anymore.

The Woman as Figure

Why, when I see the child
walking with the woman at a little distance
from the blowing trees, see the pale blue figures
of the fog, and the patches of light like just-opened
passages on the sea, does my mind veer
to violence, why then do I think something terrible
is about to happen, and why do I think the woman
has known this all along, and is waiting for it to begin,
the blows and the harsh breathing and the cries
of accusation and helplessness? I think
I am being used by something violent and merciless,
and I can't think of a way to make
this perception believable or pertinent, the way the woman,
entering a church to get out of the rain,
will shake the water from her hair
and look around her at the ornately extruded display,
the tons of bullion, to find a point of simplicity,
maybe the embroidered hem, maybe the soft curve
of a saint's elbow, maybe the single sliver of bluish light
falling across the back of a man knelt
praying, and take this into herself,
as one would take a small piece of treasure
offered in passing by a king, who himself,
worried and overcome by the problems of the state,
dreams of a garden, the one he knew as a child,
where he walked among the long hesitations of twilight,
planning battles and gaily painted ships
on fire and death sentences only he could rescind.

The Fiddler

You ride around the country in an old car,
stopping at beat-up motels, stepping into Nebraska
as one would step onto a white ferry,
hoping to meet someone who wants to be touched
all over, who wants to touch you. The sun
lowers itself calmly down the sky ropes, and
as the day ends, you put certain questions to yourself,
the smart ones about the meaning of things,
the dumb ones about the blister inside your elbow,
and if someone comes up to you, you try not
to be too romantic about it, you don't pull back
or crank up a posture that obliterates whatever
might come next; you tell a little story about the place
you come from, back East maybe, or down South,
you say something about the bird you caught
on a fly cast, how once, on fall's second day,
the grass turned white with frost; you angle in
slightly, as anyone would, nudging yourself toward more life,
like an otter or a purple martin might, or anything
breathing; and you remember your mother, the fiddler,
the summer night thirty years ago after your father
almost killed her, and how you waked under the
pasty stars to hear her playing in the dark, some old song,
sustained and elegant, that no one but her knew the name of.

The Palms

When the sun went down in L.A. that day I was driving
a rental car east on Sunset Boulevard,
worn down by the endless internal battering,
and looked back to see the vivid capacious burned oceanic light,
the dust in the air that made the light palpable and beautiful
hanging over the pastel city, and saw the crunched little stores
with their brocades of steel locking them up
and the narrow streets springing downhill like madmen
running away; and there was a ridge that blocked the sun,
a scruffy torn wall of yellow earth with a few small houses on top,
widely spaced, disconnected-looking, though down from them
there was a neighborhood of bunched-up shacks
and a street that wound through patches of willow and bouganvillea;
and on the ridge that was sharply defined by the
rotted unmanageable light, there were a few palm trees,
untouched at that moment by breeze so that their tops
hung limply; and they seemed, black against the huge sky
of Los Angeles, like small dark thoughts tethered
at the end of reason's thick ropes, hanging there in gratuitous solitude,
like the thoughts of a man behind a cluttered restaurant counter,
who speaks no English, wearing a hat made of butcher paper,
who slaps and slaps his small daughter, until they both are stunned,
stupid and helpless, overwhelmed by their lives.

Figurative Marriage

Something so mixed, almost apparent
among my wife's new clothes swinging on hangers
in the bathroom, the package of worn-out garments

wrapped like a gift in newspaper that I carry downstairs,
thinking of those windless, cool days in early spring
just before desire takes over again, before even the violets

pop their latches and the colorful slick birds
reappear from Florida. Downstairs the young couple
argue in front of their store, which is not doing well;

they look as if they don't know each other: his dark face
set against her pale one, their hands underscoring
separate facts. Oh, I figure they'll work it out,

they will not launch off alone so soon into the darkness
and disorder of the world.
                                    I know what it is to sit

late in a restaurant, each passerby an affront
and a hope unrealized. I could take you down to the end
of the street where I waited for the weather to change,

for the slack snow to turn to rain and then to sunlight,
a few days of sun bringing a slight uplift to the spirit.
I don't think it does any good to complain about this world,

its arrangement of miseries and misfires that go on
snapping off the ends of things like a machine left
running. Even the monks say the idea is to keep

going, though they are only soldiers, who must be roused
and pointed to the battle.
                        Already this season the days

are long, the fresh sunsets spectacular in reds and regal
grays. The fishermen on the river have switched baits,
replacing lures with mottled pieces of fresh squid; they rise

to the work, often solitary in small boats, dark
against the lighter dark of trees on the far shore,
their eloquent movements an abstract or diagram

of movement, of the cast-forth and draw-back that is a figure
we all recognize. Watching them I think how often I learn
something about myself in the smallest motion of a stranger,

from old men complaining at the newsstand, from the face
and hands of the solitary woman cleaning a small spill
of coffee from the radiant Formica, arranging a place for herself

in the world, settling into it, buttering carefully the small toast,
touching the knife to the grain of the bread, raising the knife
to lick avidly the fat greasy gold of butter, until it is clean.

Omnipotence

I wanted to see the emotion in my brother's face
the night his child was born, I wanted tears, the face
red and beaten and his wife gray and nearly dead
in the ripped sheets and the baby slick
from the gushed oils of the body—I was glad my brother
couldn't take the birth and ran outside
to vomit into the gardenias and the midwife ordered
him to stay there and his wife screamed and choked
and screamed for help and my brother fell to his knees
in the yard praying or crying and the storm whipped
the chinaberries and made the fence wire sing and
the old house thumped and thudded against itself
as the crying and the screaming went on until
dawn when as the gray streaks raised themselves
like Hercules lifting the night off I saw
the ground littered with blue flowers and my brother
soaked to the skin slumped against the side of the house
while the midwife, tense on the steps, looked down at him
holding herself in bloody arms apologizing.

The Exile's Daughter

The Chinese eating soft-shell crabs
are lazy in the lazy light of velvets
and red banquettes. They drink
and sing an anthem of the old lost days
and weep. I remember weeping with
Matsumoto, Korean farmer, years ago,
in his kitchen by the pepper fields,
as his crazy daughter peeped at us
from the door. She wore bright blue panties
and carried coral rocks, and her slender body
was streaked with mud as if mud was paint.
Matsumoto closed his eyes
and sang the anthem of his country
lost. Yokohama vodka gleamed in pools
on the table, like oil. Beyond
us in the burly tropic night
owls called across the bamboo glades.
A war was on. Drunk,
we'd stagger out to shout at planes
that strafed in memory
or dream. The kitchen's canvas roof
glowed like fire. Arm in arm
we'd stumble in the pepper rows
and fall. Droughty dust, like our
own thoughts pulverized, stained our skin:
the world, the world we knew, was sick of itself;
it struck itself like a man in a fit,
like Matsumoto's daughter crouching near us
in the shredded pepper vines, who struck

her face with rocks and
howled out loud at the clean and faithless stars,
and crawled up to us where we lay
and licked our faces like a dog.

Jackplay

The cars debouching from the black tunnel mouth
bear down on us here,
stranded on an island in Varick Street;
it is
like a lilac thunder, a violet
regeneration coming in over the Hudson tonight,
the light
springing back from the elaborate, sinister facades,
the streets flooding
with darkness, the gleaming red signs,
the Jamaican music, all we could ask for.
A small black and white cat
curls around the lintels of the police stable door;
there's the smell of hay and horse droppings,
I see the soft yellow light inside, it could be
Alexandrian, it could be
ancient, it
could be simply an image
or perception of warmth and another world,
as I wonder
why we sometimes need other worlds,
as even this world
with its black doors and stamped
tin cornices,
its flickering table lights
like moths hovering above the dark blue velvet
in a restaurant across the street,
is, for some,
another world, a promise,
or a promise
enacted;

as when,
at the end of evening,
lovers walk by the boat basin,
near the murk
and disaster of tides, and pause to watch
a small gathering,
a few couples eating supper
at a small table on the stern of a white yacht,
establishing in their minds an image of gaiety
and of the improbable
richness of life, though
those they celebrate are strangers,
themselves
only celebrating
perhaps the ruthless triumphs
of greed,
and of their own mortal, murderous wills.

Character Part

The aging actress makes a salad
in the sink, plunders Boston lettuce
and the dandelion greens, fingers grit
off stalks of celery, accepts the cold water,
the radishes, the purple onion chips,
the tomatoes plump and feverish, the skins
just splitting—*Tomatoed out*, the grocer
said, ripe beyond their time,
but she bought them anyway. She
believes the small work of the world
will save her for a while, believes as best
she can. There are too many memories,
too many nights alone in studios where music
played the strangulations of a fate she ardently
portrayed. Sometimes she became
the character and sensed the snake of
another's life writhing in her legs.
She remembers streets at night,
the sullen, glossy pavement
and the smells of roasted meat, shadows
in a doorway that she passed. A waiter
knew her name, and seemed,
as he arranged the heavy silverware,
to make an altar for her life.
It was quiet in the evenings there.
On Mondays she'd drive out to the beach,
never leave the car. Between the dunes
the ocean from a distance seemed undisturbed,
like remains after a struggle's passed. Later,
in her lover's arms, she'd replay the day,
taking parts, being for a while the grass,

then the heaps of petals
underneath the hedgerose banks, the sink of rain
beyond a headland in the west. Like air,
as he labored over her, she'd circulate,
touching down and leaving, praising with her touch
the green flags above the lifeguard stand,
the rocking waters, someone's name written in the sand.

Revision

Drunken brothers, they'd stagger out under the midnight
gabled fustian lights, under the milk-flecked streaks
of white cloud, to shoot crows, to shoot whatever night
flung over the house, the yard, pinched out of the sky
above the pond where the fishes sipped air, sipped bugs
at the surface and the gnat clouds wheeled like sails,
inhaling, exhaling the breath of the wind. And if
it was always summer then it was not always a night
of drunkenness and distortion, it was not always a night
when one scamp at the end of his rope turned to his
brother and accused him of adultery, of sex-love with
his—the brother's—wife, and not always a grease of love
on his hands and tufts of cow hair twisted in the barbed-
wire fence, or bare feet on the grass, the itch of wet
grass at their ankles, and the brother, driven almost entirely
mad—by lust, by loss, by alcohol—raised some gun,
some almost ancient taped-together gun, and fired, once,
three times, repealing silence and the life of his
brother, who became all at once something else, a thought
he wanted to keep to himself, a toll of flesh.

Carnivore

There is a white light
like white buck shoes standing at the glossy
end of an alley of young maples,
where just now a man, who has worked—so he thinks—
his whole life
for as nearly nothing as he can imagine,
waits. He is thinking that he will not go one
step farther, will not try
one more time to tell someone he loves her,
will not attempt to explain to his boss
or to his children that he must
lie down and rest. What could save me, he thinks,
beyond what I can picture for myself?
And what kind of world is this where I dream
of a party on a beach in some country
where palm trees dominate the landscape,
and the breezes are cool and you can see the spiny
ship masts swaying above the docks,
and the sea is so clear you can watch whatever you drop into it
fall forever through the crystal
emptiness? Now he might turn to a small
work of his hands; or he might step off the path
into the woods where a hermit thrush calls
to itself again; where the rustle among alders
is the rustle of an animal life so unfamiliar
he might as well make a fairy tale out of it,
so strange and compelling—he has stepped from the path—
that he cannot, for a couple of seconds,
think of anything else but this life—small, furred,
instinctual—of bright teeth snapping and tearing
an old piece of flesh, some partially

rotten paw or brain pan, that the animal,
this lynx or ferret,
gorges on so intensely, so obliviously. It is a minor
fantasy, a small tale he will forget
before he steps out into sunlight from this alley
of trees. Someone will call his name,
as they always do in families; someone will
ask him to stir the iced tea. He will wipe
sweat from his forehead and stop, for just a moment,
and look at his hands, as if there might be blood.

Onanism

Then she steps into me
as if I am a carcass she has gutted
and taken down from the drying rack
and stepped into: legs into legs,
arms into arms, head into head, etc.
She walks around inside me
telling everyone the secrets I've spent
my life trying to keep hidden. Later
she's tired and sits down by the river.
A scattering of white feathers
floats by. I'm lonely, she says.
Nervously, to appease her,
I begin to touch myself everywhere.

The Missing Person

You've taken to the church at last,
and tell me of the golden ritual
and sin's sweet expiation; we
both hear it's commonplace, grown men
reaching back, putting on the robes,
the silky hats, kneeling in velvet pews
they hated years ago. That year we
drove the longhorn steers in Mexico,
boys riding herd through stony wilderness
of cactus and creosote, we carried what
we needed as we went. A cloud, sunset
framed on brassy rims, was drama to us
then, so sketchy the world, so simplified.
When your spotted mare foundered
in a ditch, you cried; the days
were a single pebble turned to a new face.
Now your life's too much. Now you need
another dimension. I would join you
I suppose it'd do me good. But I can't
see the shimmer of the spirit leaping
like a flame across the scarlet folds.
Nor hear the missing person calling
from the hymn. You say you're calmer
now and know repose. At evening
when you look out at the docks,
the polished pleasure yachts excite
you still, but now you see them on
the darkened tossing plain of seas as
metaphors, and not as white ships going down.

Redneck Riviera

We ate at a poor restaurant
that was brightly lit and where the waitress
who was new at the job
tried hard to get our orders right
and brought a piece of streaky fish
that was tough and tasteless while around us
sunburned families from country towns in Alabama
and south Georgia ate the same food
without saying much
to the waitress or each other.
It was such a starry night
and we were such a long way from home,
still so shaky with each other
after the scare of our marriage falling
apart, that I leaned over and kissed
you on the mouth and tasted the lemon
and the dry baked fish
like ashes on the lips of the dead.

Lies to the Dying

Today we are going into shelter,
we are going underground to discover the passage that leads
to the next world. We will be happy there,
or we will not worry about happiness; we will make clean designs
in skin and wool, emblems we set against the stone walls
for posterity to find. Today I picture the generations
of our kind, crossing the marshy bridge into this country,
picture the long ramble down the icy, scoured valleys,
and I wonder what made them do it, without philosophy
or belief, without even much they wanted from the earth.
I see them haggard at the edge of a muddy wallow,
their minds like notches cut into stone, the stick
they fling a kind of miracle, a glance like a handful of fire
tossed in the air, no language to back them up. Today,
from the suburbs, I salute them, as if I am drunk
and falsely exuberant, as if I am just leaving the house
of a friend who is dying, who has dragged her bed
under the window to watch the ordinary street pass by.
I could tell lies to the dying, it would be easy,
easy to say that we are at the beginning, not at the end,
that all the business in the swamps with cutthroat beasts
was only prologue, as Homer was prologue,
as Dante and Stalin and your Aunt Edna were prologue,
that the trek is just getting under way here
as we flash our knives and call
over the "great distances of our longing"
promising to love each other the way we promised.

Let us think now of our lives, drifting in spirals of yellow weed,
and the islands, fragments merely, sea-washed, grass-haired,
giants standing to their brows in the sea, twirled in the sun . . .

•

Someone will create from your lives a story that tells
a truth you were waiting to hear, that is nothing like
the truths we learned in our days of power;
he will use other domesticos, other quick, toothy animals,
another lover or two, thinking beasts, a white-haired woman
squatting at the edge of a grassy pond
perhaps, or someone no one can think of now,
and from this you will begin to encounter, deep in your bodies,
the movement of another time and place,
the movement in another part of your brain
that you confuse with heart or spirit.
You will step out under the scarlet starfire
and stand there holding someone in your arms
whom you can't even imagine now,
ready for the next terrible venture, for the next slagheap
to climb and clamber over the top of singing
or crying, forcing your pity into the lives of your friends,
taking in your skinny arms one more time these bent
and troubled creatures, these midgets and posturers
dripping stinks their fathers tried to forget,
smashing your fists into the face of all that you love.

The Day Race

The small race quite furious and sustained,
as love sometimes is,
the dull, half-crumpled cars flinging
the metal-shouldered flesh into the far turn.
We are high up, regal and furious,
delighted, spoiled by dust and division,
by the battering tumble beyond which,
beyond tin fences and gates and the brash bleachers,
the fields lie naked in the sun,
green and a fatty yellow
streaked with flashes of white flowers
called woolyheads. I am gripped and entranced,
like a boy drowning at his baptism, trailing
the thick bronze hair of the woman
I love. Cars jostle and collide,
someone spins out rudely, crashes; sheets,
torn metal messages whirl upward
as the car comes to rest against the gapped white fence,
depleted, ruined,
the whipped driver staring into
the dull yellow fields. Who knows
the end of things
before it comes? Who can gauge
and guess the trivial masterpieces
we cling to like an old house
our mother died in years ago?
The roar is tremendous,
it stuns the steel pylons, tears waves
and unseen rudimentary monuments
like visions hovering and
humming near the elaborate clouds; river gulls

ride on it. Self-knowledge
and the knowledge we earned
fumbling at the ripped edges of our lives
are often not enough; skin tears,
the mind wavers and drifts,
races faster. I give love its due
and tremble, sometimes taking sides
against myself, sometimes entering,
as a man enters the dark hall of his own house,
the means of others. Now the cars,
fierce-faced like shamans,
appear at the turn four abreast
and for many this noisy rush and pursuit
is vital. They give their whole hearts
to it, almost helplessly
like children eating stolen pies.
I can see the slim form, the face
of the woman I love,
whom I will take into my arms later
and hold against loss
or against nothing but the compulsion
to do this, making her way
with discrete courtesy through a crowd of strangers.
Soon the air will catch fire
and some of us will learn,
warming our hands at the side of a vehicle
carrying us into the new ranges
that were here all the time,
that we do better among others,
are in this way not so strange to ourselves,
will learn that love takes place among the flesh

and the simple reasons
everyone understands. The race blares
and scatters; there are those who love speed,
who love the wild thunder of the cars
bearing down on us here; who love
the soft lunacy of silence that comes soon enough
out of the windy trees
and the end of things; who love the momentary hopes,
often unfounded, the possibility of peace
that drifts oddly and unsuspected
out of the bright flashings. Now we rise to our feet screaming,
alive, as we always were, at the heart of the world.

Amnesia

It's amazing
to think you can make trees
take part in this, the way, say, in north Florida
you can walk out into the pasture and say look at that:
the live oak branches slung so low
the trees seem to be squatting;
                                   and the patches of rainwet
streaking the backs of thoroughbreds
gathered near the fence can remind you of snow
drying on blankets outside a house in New Mexico,
that spring you climbed into the mountains,
arguing the whole way with your first wife, who, dumbly,
in the last spasm of her tolerance, hung her head
and pretended to listen.
                         Now everything
seems to circle back; old faces appear
among faces on the street, the unnameable trees
you passed each day
are only, someone says, Bradford pears,
common now in the minds of developers, fruitless,
as dark and glossy as the trees of legendary
kingdoms, but common.

                         Down the hill from here
the ex-President has built a library
shaped like the first letter of his name.
It is surrounded by cultivated gardens
in which young willows pick up the small castoffs
of the wind, and in the crab apples the rouged fruit
sways with a delicacy
that is nearly erotic.

Or so you might say,
coming to yourself like a man shaking off amnesia,
confused slightly
by the amiable familiarity of this world,
where just now beyond the planes and granite
angles of this monument to power and persistence,
the descendant sun selects its favorite grove,
touching it here and there lightly like a bride.

On Hearing That a Hurricane
Has Veered Toward the States

This far away, and upstairs,
I can't recognize the signs,
though the light this morning has changed,
both softer and clearer
in the quiet amber space among the elms.
There is a stillness, a momentary poise:
the loose damp grass, the bent apple trees
overloaded at the tops, the distant line of blue
mountains, do not exactly hover,
but seem perhaps to wait, perhaps not.
A listless, ordinary variety
swells the day, like the casual hum of bees;
a workman waves from a rooftop. In Jamaica,
the streets are flooded, families crowd the shelters.
You could go there in a plane
and walk among bright shanks of tin,
the torn trees; you could find the local hospital
and sit late beside a bed reading Chekhov
out loud, and stop, and touch the arm of one
whose life is changed, and drift to the window
to see the faint, irregular lights
marking the town. You could smell
fresh-turned earth, the sea salt,
and other smells, worn rubber and chemicals,
rancid cotton oil. The stars on such a night
are a white shower frozen in place,
and the rattling wind in the palms
is part of a story that is the same story
you told yourself once, long ago,
as you watched a fire truck with men on it
laughing, turn the corner in front of your house,

and you saw in your mind not a house
or a neighborhood on fire, but a great field of grass,
a prairie burning under a violent blue sky,
an emptiness of space and columns of smoke
rising like towers, obscuring the sun.

On my windowsill are three spruce cones.
A pine warbler calls from the trees; the elms
are shaggy with fox grapes, the thin beady clusters
sour, food for the birds. Dew on the paths,
on the pale, yellow petals of a flower I saw by the lake.
Now the sun stumbles from the pines, a brown bird in its mouth.

The Shaved Dog

Unreasonable moments, like the dog's hair,
shaved and hand-swept against the steps
as my father pauses to look into the springy yard,
to stare into his past that has become his future

and will provide, so he thinks, the commentators
at his death. Spring pops up
like an old habit; the dog cringes, afraid of life now,

half-sized against the breeze
that continues to blow off the lake—and my father,
who has lurched this way and that, looking for a life
that would unfold casually,

gorgeously in his two hands, stares straight into the bin
of his memory, giving himself a break,
trying to give everyone a break and failing at that,

coming, as he holds the shaver like a hilt,
to suspect that we believe certain ideas because it is too difficult
to believe others; nothing more than that,
as if the grand, Eolithic progress could be random

or more of a mystery than it already is.
You know how life grabs us up like stumbling children,
and carries us on,

and how we wake one afternoon from a nap
in a hotel in Portland, remembering someone we loved
realizing how deeply we loved; and how what it means to live
is to let the past go, to bless it or curse it,

and let it go;
and how even the death of one we loved
fades until it too is a part of the glow

surrounding us as we sit on the steps
letting the sun address us.
I know now that my father, who has been dead
half my life, wished for a death like stepping through a door,

a door that he would stand at shyly
and raise an affectionate hand
to wave us good-bye, and I believe he thought of this,

stranded on the back steps after shaving the brindle
and white hair of the mongrel dog
who lived with us then. I think as the car
plunged off the road, and the great tree rose

like the memory of his own father dark in a dream,
that his life,
that by anyone's measure

failed continuously, did not bite at him then,
but leaned back gratefully into him as one would lean back
under the sunshine of spring's first warm day.
But there is no way I can know this for sure

as my own life, lived longer than his, in a time of terror and shame,
jostles its way to the grave, like the dog's and the day's,
and the memories like fresh sheets

swung out cleanly over the old bed I lay myself down in and sleep.

The Dogwood Tree

Just beyond the summer house
I reach above my head to pull down
strings of flower mesh, vines
corroded in the castor trees, ropes of reddish
blooms, something mad,
a chaos of growth, it's out of hand.
This is something country people know about,
know the bamboo eating up the lawn,
beggar lice, thistles
rancid in a ditch, and yet we go there, we drive
straight west for fifty miles
and stumble from the car crying out our hearts of woe
among the cottonwoods, we rip a stem of fennel out
and smell the licorice in our nose, we say
the vacant places
haunt me;—we hear the wind
carping in the balsam woods,
we hear the wind changing clothes inside the laurel slick,
we say *mercy*, knowing all the time
the progress of the woods
isn't progress it's return; they are heading not toward the pikes
and package stores
but straight, "like an arrow shower," into space.
It's emptiness they want, revision,
these trees, these yellow glassy brand-new leaves,
these catkins made of yellow hair, they want—
not want; they are—dismemberment, the random
breaking up—as when the cruise ship warps away
and the clownish crowd
begins to break apart, each member absolving
himself of congregation, to become the solitary soul

who slides into the hot and dusty car, jams a tape into the box,
and idles slowly home
as Billie Holiday sings about the child she never was . . .
—they want themselves alone. They tell not of gathering,
though you know they are gathered, arranged by momentum
and the way we look at things,
into groups—they want
the old ways, the darkness,
their seeds are like atoms—it's
the darkness beyond the sleekest trunks
that gives them all away,
the silence, on a sunny day,
of shade, the way—you remember this—
when your car broke down in rural Tennessee,
and you walked along the road toward you hoped a town,
and the road sank down
onto its knees beside a stream,
and the oaks hovered darkly in the air,
the way the blossoms of a solitary dogwood tree
that hung above the scattered grass,
the freshened white disorder, colloquial as spit,
walked straight into your body,
and cleared you out of everything you held in ransom there.

The Hour of Our Birth

This slaughterhouse, this Versailles—how easy
to make claims, as another man, in another time,
dismembers his mother, in homage, in brilliance,
in stupefaction as rich as the bulky mutual anguish
of his birth hour: the dumb avidity, the breath
like cold liquid fire poured down his throat, the first
breath containing all of life, each breath after only
a repetition, a reprise: he stuffs her hands in his pockets,
steps back, sways—it is night, stardust—: "Take your hands off me,"
he says, laughs, catches a glimpse of his face in the window
and stares: Whose blood, whose pure excellence exhibited here,
what face is this that would know everything, see clearly?

Two

White Shining Sea

Thinking all day about white things,
can't get the reefed dogwood blossoms
of childhood out of my head, white ships
in a downtown boat basin, and this morning
a silent early spring snow, loose flakes
as large as dandelion cotton mingling with
pear blossoms—I used to think, whenever
the natural world unstalled and clicked
lightly through its changes, I should
tell someone, someone I loved, show her
the winter geese digging in the reeds,
the weasel den littered with fish bones
and smelling of fish—enhance life through
engagement, the hope that two could love
each other through seeing the same
remarkable moment in the same way, but now
I don't care so much . . . But what is this
love all day of white things? No power
surely in an image so simple, the
rudimentary white duck-down pillows I
remember drying on a porch rail, my
father's white shirt shining like a
breastplate—these could be any memories,
and are easily set aside for others.
I remember lying drunk in Yap across
white stones that spelled the island's
name in ancient language; the stones
bowed my back though I was too far gone
to notice. All next day I walked bent
into a stoop, and lay under a blossoming
bush looking out to sea. The flowers

smelled sweet, weren't white; the ocean
flashed and toiled without connective
power; for a second there—it was getting
late—I lost my grip, and things went blank.

The Viewing

My wife, the night her father died,
left alone in the front room with the body,
where the porch light turned glass beads
sewn into the curtains into marred jewels,
and she could hear kids yelling in the street,
and later, after it got quiet, and the house
and the street and the town, and all that part
of the country, all the way to the ocean
banging black and senseless and unappeasable
against the basalt cliffs, got quiet,
so she could hear nothing but her blood
fizzing in her ears like radios in space,
climbed on top of her father's body,
straddled it in the quiet, and in the stillness
of the single amber light, and in the stillness
of memory or desire for something more
than death had shown her already—heart attack
like a bullet between the ribs—bent low,
and opened her father's eyes with her thumbs,
to see the chalky, flattened pupils
of a dead man, to see what death looked like,
to be amazed at life, now flown.

Still Winter (Spring)

A warm, cheap snow, lightly wind-twirled,
rises (so it seems) from grates, puffs
out trees, fills the complicated furrows
of a woman's hat; it's all right to see
the worst reduced, as this snow is, to a
clumsy silliness no one could die from
or give up life distractedly sighing in,
but how close we are (still winter) to
what's merciless, as some whisper in the
happiest times: even this if walked into
steadily, boots soaking through, eyes
filling with white, could bring us down,
as something will, we who thought we
could endure anything, and almost did,
as everyone almost did, but didn't, as
spring, that staggers as it walks among
the cold stench of bodies and brisk
heartless blooms, the damp gaps
between the aging trees, reveals.

The Bad Daughter

Pale blue clouds over the stockyards
like the pale blue ragged curtains in my mother's bedroom
the year after she went crazy, living in the big house
like someone completely alone, desperate for love,
which came out the afternoon I brought her a painting,
a chocolatey, murky spellbound piece I had made,
and she came on to me madly with her eyes lit up,
her mouth out of focus, begging me to make love to her
as I had always wanted to do; and it killed me
because I wanted strength and stability after all, intimacy
after all, and saw how much she wanted it too, willing
to make me a lover, to break down anything to get there,
touching me as she trembled and wildly promised everything,
raving in the inexplicable peril she had been locked into,
like a bad daughter, high in an old house,
staring forever at the stockyards reeking of torn bodies
between her and the distant entirely untroubled bay.

The Ecstasies

I don't know about these animal bodies,
these squirrels or bird bones
that drop from the trees, or these sailors
drifted from numbered houses in the Midwest
having the time of their lives. I'm thinking
of my mother as usual, wishing she was still
with us, pondering all the good things we might
say to each other
if we were young and I was her tootling lover
arm in arm twirling along
the brazen avenues. I go straight up
out of myself sometimes like a rocket pilot,
I can't help it; I am sure by way of this
that there is more to life than we want
to admit or know, though, as always,
substance without form
is unseemly, and, at bottom,
incapacitating. I don't know why
I insist on talking in this arch
and mocking way, but I will tell you
I have watched the white yachts lumber
like polar bears into their winter berths,
and I have friends in faraway countries
who are having trouble getting a handle on things;
it is well known that I have written masterpieces
on the back of my wrist, and so what
if I am shorter than yesterday, I can ride
the tall elevator into your arms
higher than suicides climb (little
cherubs they are, bouncing and splattering,
taking it back all the way down).

"Out of Bitterness
Comes Praise"

I

Sometimes a good man wanders off,
he slips away into the traditional
desert, traveling alone through the
busted towns where at night plums
drop on the tin roofs making a sound
like madness sending a wire, and
young people sit up in the dark
counting the years of their lives,
offering dumb, grandiloquent promises
to themselves. There are places
he wanders by where a man who's
given up on everything else climbs
the raw brown hill behind his house
to chisel his dead wife's name
into the splintery rock, and the
postmistress leaves the mail in
its canvas sack and goes home to
lie in her darkened bedroom thinking
about her childhood among the poor
in Delaware. She hears wild birds
crying and dreams she is riding a
white train across the prairie
toward a town built of colored silk,
and considers the shallowness of
memory, how hope leads to desire
and back again, thinking of chickens
pecking at the rain, sleeping as
the man who is forgetting everything
he knows passes by, noticing only

the willows by the dry stream, a
girl clutching a doll on a porch
waving at something he can't see.

I I

Sometimes a man feels the desert
gather around him like leaves
blown into his yard, and he takes
a shovel and begins to dig in the
soft dirt under the copper beech,
and hides something there that
the next day he's forgotten about.
That night he tells his wife a
story about the time he lived in
Venice as a boy and watched the
green banner of a wisteria vine
climb the house across the canal,
and this story is a lie that amazes
him as he tells it, wondering how
he could think of such a thing,
but all the next day the story
repeats itself, until he believes
it is a memory from another life,
or he believes he has forgotten
the facts of his own life, until
he is so unsettled he sits in a
café crying into his hands, won-
dering who he is and what it is
about the world that dazzles so

despite all he knows. Weeks later,
after a thousand miles, he has
forgotten the story because now
there are a hundred stories he
is telling himself, one after the
other, and each story is farther
from the life he has lived and
knows, each has its moment in
which something small and bright
slides out like a snake wearing
a suit made of mirrors, and now
the towns, the desert towns propped
in dust by the dry rivers, whisper
in the darkness he passes through,
until he wonders if he will ever
believe anything again, the way he
did somewhere back in the other world
when he watched a boy in a café
drinking a cup of chocolate, and
for an instant saw the boy's life
standing before him like a god.

Some Don't Go South

Some don't go south for their health,
and some don't go at all; some squat
in scaling brick houses by cemeteries
complaining loudly, but even the worst,
the most frightened, love their kids,
each has a general idea of what life
is about, and will say it, or use it
to run things through, like a grater
tearing cheese; and some are glad to
live where they were born, and some
want to go back there, some remember
on off winter days the pile of lank
gray clouds over the Gulf, the supple
brown reeds backed into the bay's lap;
and some, who are forcing themselves
to go on with things, think force is
all, and some taking orders say this
is the way it's always been, but even
the green haze of spring settling into
the mouths of rivers, and the girl
going crazy with life, bespeak another
configuration, though by then it is
very late, and another year is passing
into what we've forgotten; the white
dock tilted over the tide, the brassy,
secular stink of the sea that transforms
the dead that somehow appear in mind,
appear only occasionally now, as what
was once the vivid, oiled body of love
cannot reclaim what it once took as a
right, something that runs away into the
mossy fog, that we are no longer sure we saw.

Ice

Torn white flaring heat smoke, tipped
flaring, like the contents of cuspidors
tipped from the roofs—smokestacks, chimneys—
of old grained buildings, shines intricately,
backlit and ice cold in January morning
sun that we go out into begging warmth from
tightened coats and scarves: the little
dogs are all puffed up and the pigeons are
puffed like shock or ruined kings strutting
in exile: "Winter from now on," someone says,
meaning the next few months, but speaking
dramatically, as we all do, as the earth does
and can't help: it's dangerous and scary
sometimes, and all the time for some, even
in dreams a tide rolls up the green river-
bank, and the loved face shrieks, so like
the shriek draining the alley last
night as we walked away from each other
dumbly and defeated into a world of ice.

Off-season Repairs

When you told me of coming down
off the roof in hurricane, all alone
in the summer island's fall, and
the wind thrusting at the sea, shingles
moaning, and out on the beach foam
piled like mattress stuffing, and
the cops winding sirens inside their
boarded station houses took over
your job, you said your shirt came loose
and you let it go, stood half-naked
in the tremendous breeze and rain
until you remembered the distant place
you'd come from, pecan trees and
smoky days, a long, carved balcony
that overlooked the sea, and there,
as you were torn, the people of that
place seemed strange, and disconnected
from the world that passed them by
all day out on the roads, and then
you seemed detached from two worlds
at once, a stranger working on a roof,
replaced by wind, and a stranger
who could hardly see her misty starting
place, and you could not hold on to
either, so you said, as you pounded
me into your body like a nail.

The Vivisectionist

The night my husband killed me I thought I was by myself.
Come in from the hunt, from grave robbing,
dragging the streaky, milky corpses, winching
them onto the kitchen table, he sweated from his work
and went to work. That night I walked in the yard
under a shower of stars, whole constellations, galaxies
coming apart, racing toward earth. You could smell
the desert, sulfurous in the heat, metallic,
like a sword rubbed against stone. I never heard him
approach, felt the prick of the blade then nothing.
How is it now I wake? Where am I now?
The light itself seems solid, though forms pass through it.
Now he slices me chin to groin, lifts my blue guts out.
I feel his big hands inside my chest.
My legs and arms become the legs of a table
he eats his breakfast on. He wears my backskin for a cape.
My head's a lamp he reads by late at night.
Through empty sockets I watch him turn the pages of his book,
and wonder what it is in there that makes him giggle.

Winter Door

The days that get away
are on my mind, how many
get away, and how, for
some, they all disappear,
like this murky fall
tailing into winter gloss,
and names of those I
said I'd love forever
that now I can't recall.
The trees are porches
to the wind, unfinished;
just yesterday I stood
outside the rugged
garden edge and watched
the wind press down
the tawny grass like
a current racing on the
bottom of a shallow sea,
but not a sea because
a trembling moving light
accompanied it, a surge
of brief, flashing strokes
that seemed alive, more
alive than grass, which
was lank and bent. I'm
troubled by some harm
I've caused and can't,
or won't, redress, and I
wish it didn't take so
long for the truths I
claim to become the

truths I live. The meager
sun across the naked
branches seems to skitter,
seems to fray; at times,
like a backward glance
I've remembered all these
years, too much is clear.

Country Weekends

Clouds like a series of uncomplicated
elegies, or remnants of an awkward
discussion that'll be continued later,
and couples, come up for the weekend,
ply their hosts with questions, performing
a selection of vague maneuvers they've
worked out in advance; the lake takes
on a black enamel sheen, and even the
crests and pockets of water plants,
leaftops shaped like utensils you'd
find in any good kitchen or gardening
shed, deepen in color, seem to thicken
and swell, as the world or one's good
intentions expand today toward cool
rain pressing in over the mountains.
Sometimes there's no mystery at all,
about things, only the wired-up, mostly
uncomplicated devices we use to fool
children, a certain sweet taste in
the mouth left over from lunch, and
then the same couples who might have
divorced yesterday, if divorce were as
easy as breaking a stick, trotting off
to sunny bedrooms for a nap. The
women speak of their dreams, and the
men, walking under the trees, stop
to throw rocks, measuring distances;
after drinks, supper, and talk, the
house will grow quiet; a snatch of
laughter, the smallest, keenest of
cries, and a parcel of tears, delivered

from an otherwise ordinary past, will
be left on a pillow. Someone passes
under the window whispering secrets,
cursing the angles that crack as
they close; we can't quite hear,
and then there is nothing to hear.

The White City

The morning is smudged and still,
heavy with unspent rain. The light
quiets prismatic colors, brings
out grays and near blacks,
swells the white side of a house
with subcutaneous fat until it
shines. The wet street gleams.
And the smooth and the furrowed
branches gleam, and the manhole
covers gleam like blisters. Two
concrete dogs, painted gray, like
ship's fixtures, and a gray cat
in the window of the Nepalese shop
stare into the dim street. How
often a given day brings us to
the threshold of something weighted
and nearly absolute, a city
foundered, love spent; so many
times—clouds quilted and swollen
as if they enclose other clouds
or thick mysteries that can't be
revealed—we grow used to it, or lose
interest, as the sooty day drains,
and the doctor, come at last,
presses the girl's slight hand that
is growing pale as he holds it.

To Lautreamont

I don't know what to say to you
and have called you names—mutilator of souls,
warden of dust, evocator—that only placed me
at a disadvantage. I turn my sweet gaze
away and lose you, I fall in love with small
women selling curios, and come to in white rooms
high above the city to the sound of faint
music and a child crying. Why are the walls
rubbled and muddled like the walls of caves?

I forgot you at times, chased wounded birds
into the thickets, small, yellow-eyed hawks
and less important creatures, and it was
not only from despair that I stayed away
from your palaces: I came to love the woods
and the small declivities in which cool
water stood calmly as if sleeping.

I am afraid all the time but go on anyway;
I speak loosely, as one who was familiar
with grandeur, but it is in the simple
sadness of twilight that I am most useful;
it is there, as you have taught me,
that I can be appreciated as one for whom
the soft struggles of reason give way
to a shoddy but pleasing invention.
I hope that the carved sticks of my will,
broken so often and useless now, might appeal
to you, and these worn tales of romance,
these weasels and mice I have tracked
to their dens and befriended, won't offend.

You are on my mind always these days,
always in the high cavities of the wind
I hear you now; some say you are near,
they say it is as if no time has passed,
they say you were on your way all along.

Chinese New Year

I

Cool spring, and a fine freshness,
burred and fruity airs along Canal,
and a dimpled face, scowling then
smiling, looks out between gold Buddhist
portals where for a dollar you get a
scroll that tells what's coming this
year—and into this year I go empty-handed
forward as a man goes into sunny fields
of wheat, fortuneless but happy, like
a man coming to on a beach in Africa,
who gets up into the squalor and stink
and begins to make a little home for
himself among the shrubs and palm
flowers; like a man who stands up in
a field of poppies and looks around,
remembering how it was to fall in love
and go gamely on with everything,
and how her breath smelled of almonds,
and how the moon shone on her breasts,
and how he thought he was getting
somewhere at last and stood outside
shops in Chinatown stunned as she tried
on jeweled slippers, pair after pair—

I I

and the year that rises, like a vanished
continent the sea ebbs back from, sprawls

naked before me in patches of rose
and gold, and I hear the voices that
live in the shapes and gestures of the
dense world around me, the silent voice
of a boy climbing the dark stairs at the
back of a house, and the voice of the bird-
wing fan the girl going alone into her
future brings to her lips and kisses, as
she will kiss, years from now, the face
of the man who loves her; and I hear
the soft singing, like radio waves
stained by plum flowers, going on
behind the bins and catchments brimming
with trash; and out on the river where
the stars float all night on their backs
looking up at themselves, the foghorn
solemnly cries, like an owl, or like one
so struck by life he must steadily repeat
the moment of grace that is neither warning
nor welcome, but the passing and figure
of time itself, the chipped figure
standing in the shallows of night, singing.

Lower Fifth

In light yellow leaf mist
the trees take shape, iterate
form before form, semblance
before fact: and the boxed
sun, shackled and dully
gleaming like sanded copper,
fills the memorial arch
that looks from Thirty-Fourth
Street—downhill—like a reef
or fortress gate thrown
open onto an undifferentiated
world, a curved space like
desert or a blank field
of light, past which there
is nothing at all but
thought itself, irreducible
and without form beyond
what the clean shape of
its enabling frame makes
of it, an emptiness not
contained but looked out
on, and by those traveling
toward it, steadily into.

The Children's House

Summery declarations, proposed now above yellow frost
    glistening on the ivy beds, father assembles
the baroque, sophisticated children's house the girls
    will play in, heated, lace in the eaves, colander
windows like bubble eyes he always wanted to look out of;
    and the girls, rising early, see it in the dawn light
like the ship that is bringing the prayed-for supplies
    to the elaborately dressed, dying settlers—inside,
where the artificial tin stove and the blue plastic dishes
    and the pegs for hanging the toys
that are already disappearing into dreams, shine,
    they walk about in pale dresses and kneel
to accept the mind's grandiose fabrications that are like
    cakes sugary and scrolled with purple and red
words they read as charms; the world wears gold leggings
    and speaks frankly in sounds like colorful flags
snapping at the tops of slender poles, and, often,
    birds on their way south fly through, from one window
out the other like snatches of color torn from the sea
    that, later, when you lie on your back almost dreaming,
hang among the fat-lipped leaves of distant African trees.
    It is almost impossible to tell what happens
when life goes on forever this way, to even speak
    to the regal stranger dying in the doorway
who has crawled across a rocky desert to get here;
    one girl, the younger, sees a face
raised begging, and screams, but only in her mind, waits,
    lets the sun make of the future someone she loves,
as the mind, indentured to itself, will propose the same mission,
    leaning against the foreknowledge of pain

as one leans against the swaggering clown carrying
        bad children to the ships that are leaving,
though nothing ever leaves, and two neighborhood dogs,
        returned from the frontier, fiercely crooked,
bite at the base of each other's spine.

Kiss of the Moon

She tells an awkward story, about hunting
rabbits, the bleached gleam of the moon
lies in patches and long slender washes
about the room, it is late and they have
drunk wine and eaten freshly canned summer
peaches that she tastes as she presses her face
into his neck and lightly begins to bite;
he's nearly a stranger, but willing to share
the extra bed—a weekend country celebration
—he watched as she undressed in the moonlight,
thinking of the long ride tomorrow and
of his brother's tedious misery he can't
stop talking about; he was almost dreaming
just now of a flight of white ibises
rising over the pond, and of the long,
lightly ruffled bodies reflected in the
black surface; her lips are the light brush
of a bird's wing, kiss of the moon, then
the hard fracture of pain begins to sting
and it is as if the night has begun to
smother him in the thick, low smell of peaches.

Mother at Eighty

You come in dream, Mother, or not at all,
distressed by drugs, scattering quips, complaining
still about the way they torture you. Married late,
you wouldn't leave the party, forced Hawaii
to its knees; I've seen the cascades of your hair,
heard the devilish laugh each suitor ducked, ricocheting
through the rooms; a wastrel girl, uncontrollable.
And press through time to take you in my arms,
to find you now, coldcocked by suffering,
baggage in a train that's plowed its way
into the dark and snowy woods, and stopped.
I see you there, my dreamer, nodding at your window,
unacknowledged, except perhaps by the spotted dog
limping in the snow, that sees you lift your head,
and trembles in your smoky, avid glance.

Adhesion

Sweet appraisal of a touch,
and the slender form of day
the window makes, the antiquated
blue, hemmed by the yellow hill,
appear this morning like the
fastidious sisters to the brother
of my mood, shapely counterpoints
of softly dented skin and figured
sky, two surfaces exposed and
lingered over in the brief exchange
of touch for glance; the vivid
arrival of the day, your supple,
fragrant skin I press my face
into, adhere, like parts that
make a whole, like a formula
that extrudes my life; as you
cradle in my arms I watch the
breeze sip the trees, the trees
that respond to what has flown
all night to show itself, as
your subtle flesh shows itself
to me; like a silence broken.

Singapore

I got up and I wasn't feeling so good,
something was wrong that I sat on the edge of the bed
trying to figure out,
                            but I didn't really
want to know, wanted trouble simply to subside,
and watched a woman in the other building
touch and paint her face and enjoyed the delicacy
of her fingers and the smart, quick brushing
movements;

            as I looked deeper into the room
I could see a few of the items she made her home with,
the shabby excrescences and mementos
that were like my own, and then, against the gray wall,
a man lying on a bed, who was naked, and sleeping,
or maybe watching her as I was, waiting
as the night lifted for the hard-won glamour
of her face to turn toward him;

we might have been in a movie,

in some weary place like Singapore during the war,

the camera might be pulling back down the long street
the sun on summer mornings rises at the end of,

and these people who are really only strangers
the day is taking briefly to its heart
might be two I know well, two I have loved
and had rough words with and long for now,

adrift in my own troubles as I am,

and even the camera, maybe only the camera,
knows this clearly and is trying to make this clear,
rising as it does in the slow long pull of a bird's ascent
above the buildings and the trees,
drawing, so it seems, as it leaves us,
the two sides of this particular morning vista
closer together,
                    rising above everything here
until the street and the neighborhood become frets
in a pattern it is impossible to decipher,

until the city, beginning to pant in the sunlight,
becomes one more body sprawled on a plain
beside a river opening its dark hands
to the elaborate, giddy sea.

The Rose

I'm looking everywhere for new ways,
poking, selecting, looking everywhere,
turning the trees over, rummaging among skirts
and stars. I'm so lonely and intense, so
tense and energetic, I'm getting up early
to touch the slick habit of ice on the windowsill,
to touch dust and the dried blue berries of juniper.
I'm shaking and scared of life
and of the absence of life, childless, love
buried out in the prairie far from here
under the shifty grass; I'm watching the white birds
drift up from the south, reading the last lights
in the tall buildings like lines of white type
spelling the future, I'm into everything
haphazardly and wholly, revenant and pilgrim,
I'm looking as I go and I go formally and
rapidly, moving through gales of solitude,
through crowds and the cries of young children;
I'm tasting, I'm smelling everything, I'm
stooping in Chinatown to lick the boots of
the Buddhists, I'm pressing my bare skin
to the ancient stone designs of artisans lost
to the world; I'm looking everywhere, I'm alert,
I'm open like a child's blue coat as he runs,
I'm ready for bronze and happiness, I'm gamely
adjusting the water level, I'm forgiving it all,
telling it all, hearing it all, I'm ready
for fake silk patches spilling from envelopes,
I'm ready for a "vague splintering of rain,"
ready—I'm looking everywhere—for a delicate
means of transition, I'm stumbling against

beauty and not apologizing, I'm almost naked here,
skinnier than I used to be, almost helpless
or maybe I'm completely helpless as the religious
say is the way to heaven—all right I'm helpless—
I'm swaying on the platform, I'm tenderly
toasting the bread, I'm placing the saucer,
the spoon on the tray, I'm arranging the rose,
I'm pulling the curtain, I'm letting light flood the room.